Difficult Riddles: 300 Challenging Riddles That Smart Kids And Families Will Love

Jack Merrin

No part of this publication may be reproduced, distributed, or transmitted in any form or by any means, including photocopying, recording, or other electronic or mechanical methods, without the prior written permission.

© 2020 Jack Merrin
All Rights Reserved

Other Puzzle Titles
   -by Jack Merrin

1. Cryptograms: 200 LARGE PRINT Cryptogram Puzzles of Inspiration, Motivation, and Wisdom

2. Cryptograms #2: 250 Humorous LARGE PRINT Cryptoquote Puzzles

3. Cryptograms #3: 200 Philosophical LARGE PRINT Cryptoquote Puzzles

Table of Contents

Contents..............................4
Basic Riddles........................5
Intermediate Riddles...........16
Difficult Riddles..................27
Answers.............................39

Basic Riddles (1-100)

1. I have lots of teeth, but I cannot chew.
   I help people with their hairdo.

2. I can form a bubble.
   If I get in your hair, then there is trouble.

3. The king uses me to make a knight.
   I come in handy when I'm in a fight.

4. I own many needles, but I prefer not to sew.
   Underneath me is where many gifts go.

5. Half wood and half lead,
   I help things to be read.

6. In a speech, or in a song,
   which word is always pronounced wrong?

7. The more of me,
   the less you see.

8. You climb to my top and then ride me down.
   Kids use me and scream a joyous sound.

9. I have many hearts but do not breathe.
   There are many games that I do weave.

10. I have one eye, but I am blind.
    I allow particular objects to bind.

11. I have a head and a tail,
    but I am not a common animal or a snail.

12. I like to repeat what you say.
    Keep me in a cage, or I will fly away:

13. I am a country or a bird.
    My presidential pardon is quite absurd.

14. I have four legs but cannot walk.
    I am the final destination after using a wok.

15. Which planet did astronomers discover first?
    There are a lot of them out in the universe.

16. What sits standing up and loves to jump?
    It has a pouch, but not a hump.

17. I contain holes all over do you know,
    but I can easily hold H2O.

18. To ride me, a great balance is needed.
    I only spin one wheel once you are seated.

19. Parents insist you wear me,
    in the winter and fall.
    I am also used to cover a painted wall.

20. I am round but not a wheel.
    I am sometimes made out of steel.
    I grow inside every tree.
    Here, a boxing match you can see.

21. You need me to live,
    but it rhymes with the dead.
    Indeed you will also find,
    that it is the opposite of behind.

22. If you cut me, I won't cry.
    But you will. Do you know why?

23. If you don't have the cash, I can save the day.
    Expect to pay later, in an interesting way.

24. Which word in the dictionary
    is spelled mistakenly?
    Can you come up with the answer quickly?

25. Which letter in the alphabet,
    contains the most water?
    Please consider this delicate matter.

26. I guide you home on a stormy day.
    Towards your ship, I point the way.

27. I am made of white particles,
    but not sugar or sand.
    Spice up your food with me,
    so it doesn't taste bland.

28. This is difficult to take off your body,
    but easy to put on.
    Much easier to wear,
    but hard to have withdrawn.

29. We hide in the day but come out at night.
    After the sun rises, we are out of sight.

30. I grow up while I grow down.
    In the summer, I'm green.
    In the winter, I'm brown.

31. I know many words, but do not speak.
    I give wisdom to those who seek.

32. They first sailed the seas,
    but now they roam the internet.
    Whatever they can steal
    is what they get.

33. The better I am, the more I suck.
    Without me for specific jobs,
    you are out of luck.

34. I have four fingers, a thumb, and no hand.
    Tell me why, can you understand.

35. Take away some, and one remains.
    What did I start with, use your brains?

36. I am round, but something you eat.
    I am not a vegetable but made of meat.

37. Under your head,
    I listen to stories unsaid.
    In my feathery seam,
    I support your dream.

38. Make a house, a spaceship, or a castle
    with this toy.
    400 billion copies strong, I bring much joy.

39. I am able to fly without any wings.
    I am one of life's most precious things.

40. I am hated by a liar.
    Scientists for me do inquire.

41. How many months have 28 days?
    Try to think about it in several ways.

42. I have keys, but no need for a lock.
    I don't have a mouth,
    but make your computer talk.

43. Who follows you around in your hall,
    but doesn't weigh anything at all?

44. I guard your house. I'm all around,
    Half above and half below the ground.

45. I keep you cool when it is hot.
    A star needs many of these to keep on top.

46. I have a neck, but no head.
    I like to wear a cap instead.

47. You use me once, then throw me out.
    I tell you what yesterday was all about.

48. With one eye, I cannot see.
    My center is a calm place to be.

49. What weighs more, a pound of feathers
or a pound of lead?
Can you think of a way to measure
the difference instead?

50. Name four days that start with the letter T.
This riddle is as easy as can be.

51. With me, what is far away looks large.
Find me where astronomers are in charge.

52. I can be a person, place, or thing.
In a sentence, I am the king.

53. I am one part home and one part plant.
Without climbing, entering me, you can't.

54. This object is something
that belongs to you.
However other people use it
more frequently than you do?

55. This kind of soda
you are not meant to drink.
Use it for cleaning,
that should make you think.

56. Monsters love to devour me.
I go well with coffee, milk, or tea.

57. An example of me is thyme,
and I also split yearly time.

58. When I cry I make a thunderous sound,
    but afterward, I am nowhere to be found.

59. I can make you jump,
    I can apply a force.
    Made of fiber,
    I can drive a horse.

60. Food is in my stomach,
    but I don't eat.
    Get out of the kitchen
    if you can't stand the heat.

61. When I fall down, I feel no pain.
    I could fill your cup but have nothing to gain.

62. I am first on earth, and second in heaven.
    I am not in six, but twice in seven.

63. You will find tasty treasure
    in my golden center,
    but the average man
    would dare not enter.

64. What does MOM say
    when she is upside down?
    As a hint, it is a curious noun.

65. Spread me around,
    and I will keep you protected
    from the sun's rays that are projected.

66. If you give me food, then I will thrive,
    but give me water, and I cease to be alive.

67. This fish is really rich.
    Do you know which?

68. I have many keys, but doors I do not unlock.
    I make many sounds, but do not talk.

69. I am sometimes in your teeth and in your hair.
    I am necessary for proper care.

70. Once inside, you are never let loose,
    a box nobody wants to use.

71. I can go through a window if it is open or shut.
    The answer is simple, do you know what?

72. I was born on Christmas,
    yet my birthday is in summer?
    How is this possible, do you wonder?

73. If you subtract one letter
    or one number from me,
    you get something that is even
    as you will see.

74. I have hands but cannot make applause.
    I work all day and night without a pause.

75. What word becomes smaller
    when you add two letters to it?
    This one is easy,
    I must admit.

76. You give it away, but keep it at the same time.
    If you break it, that is definitely a crime.

77. These doors are always open wide,
    not found in a house, but rather outside.

78. I go in circles, but I am led.
    You can steer me left, right, or straight ahead.

79. How much dirt is in a hole that is a cubic foot?
    Think of how much dirt inside you could put.

80. I live in the rivers, the ocean, and the sky.
    When I am cold, I float. When I am hot, I fly.

81. My wings contain many stories,
    I like to share my inventories.

82. Forwards I am massive,
    and backward I'm not.
    This riddle is simple; don't think a lot.

83. I make a roaring sound.
    I make trees fall to the ground.
    Mighty jugglers wield me when they play.
    In any hardware store, I am on display.

84. I can climb a tree,
    but don't have a leg or an arm.
    If you see me, it is a cause for alarm.

85. I am white when I am dirty,
    but black when I am clean.
    I am quite an educational scene.

86. I am where you live or a type of speech.
    This is something that
    a postman must be able to reach.

87. You will find me between earth and heaven,
    as well as between six and seven.

88. Half from a husband, and a half from a wife.
    This contains all the secrets of life.

89. I carry all my property on my back.
    When I walk, I leave a slimy track.

90. An electric train goes South,
    but the wind goes West.
    What direction does the steam flow best?

91. My first part is counterfeit.
    My second part is stone.
    When I sprout four ways, I am lucky.
    This much is known.

92. If you pronounce me wrong, it is right.
    If you pronounce me right, you are wrong.
    This riddle is quite a sight.
    If you can solve it, your brain is strong.

93. I always point in the same direction.
    I am good for course correction:

94. Animals wear them on their heads.
    Humans use them with their mouths instead.

95. One in a submarine, one in a toaster,
    none in a bean, three in a rollercoaster.

96. You can't hold me for long,
    I know. I have tried.
    You can only see me,
    when it is cold outside.

97. Rearrange the letters in "THE EYES" can you,
    in order to say what they do.

98. When you become dry, I become wet,
    even though I was dry before we met.

99. Remove the whole, and some remains.
    What did I start with, use your brains.

100. I am a girl's best friend.
     In fact, on me, all life depends.

Intermediate Riddles (101-200)

101. Where does yesterday come after today?
     It is a handy place, I must say.

102. I am a kind of food or a type of speech.
     With jelly or at marriages, I work for each.

103. I am a shower but without water.
     I am celebrated in the world all over.

104. Rearrange the letters in LISTEN.
     You must be this in order to LISTEN.

105. My base is warm, and my top is cold.
     Around for millions of years, for I am old.

106. I have six faces and twenty-one eyes.
     I don't have a mouth, is that a surprise?

107. What has many a heart, but no body part?
     You can solve this if you are really smart.

108. I float but hangout mostly beneath the water.
     I go away when I get hotter.

109. I am a tree,
     but I fit in your hand.
     You will find me planted,
     where there is often sand.

110. My first part is a vehicle.
     My second part is a lad.
     I don't get paid very much,
     that much is sad.

111. I can help construct a building.
     I am also a bird. No, I'm not kidding.

112. Take 1 letter away from 6,
      and you are left with 8.
     Fat people share this common trait.

113. This is really fun.
     When is ten plus three equal to one?

114. Only six letters my word contains,
     but remove one letter and seven remains.

115. What happens a single time in a second,
     twice in a week, once in a year?
     Also, twice in a decade or once in a century,
     and the answer should be clear.

116. Think of a trunk,
     but I'm not an elephant's nose,
     part of a plant for an upright pose.

117. I flow through silver
     but not through pure water.
     I produce a current,
     but I am not a river.

118. If light shines on me, I will surely die,
     but I need light to live. Do you know why?

119. I am something you can catch,
     but you can never throw.
     I am always passed on to others, although.

120. Why can't a man living in New Mexico
     be buried in a grave in Mexico?

121. This courage comes from your back.
     Books have this to come in hardback.

122. In March and April, I happen in the middle.
     But not the begging or the end.
     Can you solve this riddle?

123. My first half is something
     you take for sickness and rhymes with ill.
     The second half is something
     near the bottom still.

124. What word starts with the letter E,
     but only contains a single letter?
     Solve this riddle when your skills are better.

125. I stay in the corner,
     but I am a world traveler.

126. My bark is worse than my bite,
     I am not allergic to light.

127. With two hands near your hand.
     Do you know what I am?

128. I can be about a person, place, or thing.
     You can find me hanging by a string.

129. I am at the end of every rainbow.
    Do you know?

130. I run on gas, and I make glass.
    I also rhyme with bass.

131. What kind of table can you eat?
    It's usually not very sweet.

132. Two coins are worth fifteen cents in sum,
    but a nickel is not one.
    What are the two coins?

133. With great writers, you will find me among.
    I am tall when I am young.
    When I am old, I am short.
    Then I can no longer help with your report.

134. I am in the window, but not in the glass.
    I am in a weed, but not in the grass.

135. The more I grow, the less you see.
    Tell me, Mr. Riddler, what could I be?

136. You play these balls in a marching band.
    The sound they make is really grand.

137. I am early in everything,
    the end of space and time.
    The start of an ending,
    and I always finish a good rhyme.

138. If I fall, it will open a big crack.
     Give me a smile, and I will give you one back.

139. You find me in a liquid but not in water.
     I am in a solid but not in matter.
     I am not in the happy but in the sadder.

140. All life starts here
     and ends with the same two of a letter.
     Get this right,
     and you will know biology better.

141. My rings are not made of gold,
     I collect more of them as I get old.

142. I like to be read,
     but I will make one more claim.
     Read me top to bottom and bottom to top,
     and you will find I am the same.
     I am different left to right and right to left,
     but not in the middle.
     This is the riddle.

143. I run all day, but don't get anywhere.
     In my cell, you will find me there.

144. I come from a tree, but I can fly low.
     Without an engine, hardly anywhere can I go.

145. I connect the earth with the sky.
     If you touch me, then you will surely die.

146. I stop you from getting wet.
     Above your eyes, you will find me set.

147. I go up as rain falls down.
     I am sold in every town.

148. First in time.
     Last in a limit.
     In this rhyme,
     and happens once in a minute.

149. I know a man who shaves ten times a day.
     But his beard is always proudly on display.
     Is there a way?

150. I am candy, but also a loving action.
     Expressing love or even passion.

151. You break me before I am used.
     This is ok. Your behavior is excused.

152. I go around the mountain
     or up and down a hill,
     yet I am completely still.

153. Donald's father has three sons.
     Huey, Dewey, and which one?

154. Molly likes steel but hates metal.
     Molly Good Golly.
     Molly likes wood but hates oak.
     Molly Good Golly.
     Molly likes apples but hates fruit.
     Molly Good Golly.
     Does Molly like hammers?

155. If I am short, then I am usually bigger,
then I am set off by the slightest trigger.

156. You can write my name by using my top row.
I am not made anymore, although.

157. I am in the group but not in the team.
I am in the thread, but not in the seam.
I am in the water and in your drink,
but you won't ever find me in the sink.

158. I have a hundred wheels or more in my spot,
would you even call this a lot.

159. What are you allowed to steal,
that helps you get closer to home?
I will give you a hint.
It's sometimes under a dome.

160. I lose my shape when I am hot.
I am malleable when I'm not.
Your secret message, I protect.
I form the house of a certain insect.

161. You can jump over this building
with a single bound.
It fades away when water is around.

162. This is where a penalty is served
and what you see
when life is microscopically observed.

163. I ask a question but never reply.
I make a loud sound, but do not cry.

164. I am the head of the committee,
     but you also sit on me.

165. I taste better than I smell.
     Don't worry. Your senses work well.

166. I am the same forward and backward.
     People call out for help with this word.

167. Whether I weigh a lot or whether I weigh low.
     My weight is the same, do you know.

168. Without me, you would have no knowledge.
     No kindergarten, high school, or even college.
     I am the tool of the scientifically gifted.
     I am one part solid and one part liquid.

169. I like to fly but never go anywhere.
     I am usually rectangular instead of square.

170. I hang out a lot on the ground.
     I never get dirty or make a sound.

171. Take a bath, and every time I shrink.
     In the water, I will sink.

172. When is 1700 + 15 equal to 1800 - 45?
     In Europe, each day, the answer does arrive.

173. I have a million eyes but am not alive.
     All my visions are recorded in an archive.

174. I come from the past, and I always last.
     I am made in the present, after what went.
     To the future I am immune,
     but I will happen soon.

175. The letters of the alphabet go from A to Z.
     Thinking what goes from Z to A is also easy.

176. The outside is green. The inside is red.
     You might want to eat it all,
     but spit out the black parts instead.

177. I am covered in bandages,
     but they don't help me heal.
     A long-time has passed since
     my last healthy meal.

178. The higher I go, the lighter I get.
     Higher than a bird, higher than a jet.

179. The colder it gets, the less I tend to wear.
     A gathering of my friends
     is a breath of fresh air.

180. You can see me again and again,
     but others cannot.
     The answer to this riddle requires
     only a simple thought.

181. Understand this riddle carefully if you dare.
     Forwards I'm a number, backwards a snare.

182. I have forests but no trees.
I have no houses, but only cities.
I have water, but no fish.
I can help you go wherever you wish.

183. Follow me around,
but I have no beginning or end.
Many have made me their sugary friend.

184. What do you call it
when you own a group of singers?
No need to count them on your fingers.

185. Remove four letters from this word,
and it sounds the same.
Like if it was one letter,
can you play this game?

186. You need this body part to live.
If you move the first letter to the last,
it describes where you live.

187. When I own this, I do not share.
If I share this, I am no longer there.

188. I am an elegant dress that can't be worn.
I can't be ironed, I can't be torn.

189. I control a lion or a tiger.
Do it to foam, and it goes much higher.

190. I am heard but not ever seen.
If you say thirteen, I will return thirteen.

191. I make two people from just one.
But also not just anyone.

192. People or dogs can catch me, but I fall slow.
I am something that you throw.

193. You answer me, but I never ask a question.
People use me, session after session.

194. I thrive in winter and die in summer.
My higher part is thicker than my lower

195. I cover your face, but you can see through me.
I am worn on happy occasions,
as well as the dreary.

196. I am the kind of light that is really bright.
Look at me, and you will lose your sight.

197. Once I am opened, I cannot be closed.
With two legs, I am composed.

198. I can cry,
but I don't have an eye.
When I am near, the farmer sings.
I can fly, but I have no wings.

199. You pay lots of cash for me,
but hope not to use me.

200. We come from a tree,
but we are not food.
We like to help you eat,
but don't taste very good.

Difficult Riddles (201-300)

201. I have an eye but can't see.
     I have no water but contain a sea.
     I make no honey but have a bee.
     No vegetables are here except for a pea.
     No need for coffee, but I enjoy a good tea.

202. If you say it, it is gone.
     You usually turn things off, to turn it on.

203. Three ways out and one way in,
     with many sizes, big, medium, and thin.

204. Many are needed to stay alive,
     but you only can play one at a time.
     It produces more of a tone,
     less of a chime.

205. Your house wears this type of clothes.
     It is something the mailman surely knows.

206. I am often overlooked.
     But with a ring, I am sometimes hooked.

207. I have two eyes, but I am flat.
     Where two sides join is where I'm at.

208. This is what you do to avoid getting hit.
     Or you can roast me on a fiery spit.

209. I never munch,
     but I always eat a light lunch.

210. I have two eyes on my head
and an eye on my tail.
The male uses them much better
than a female.

211. It is now noon, but it's dark.
Why does the sun's light not hit its mark?

212. I am what you are willing to pay.
My top and bottom halves look the same way.

213. Something that runs, but cannot walk.
Every person has one, but it cannot talk.

214. In the dark, you can easily see me,
but I am as weightless as can be.

215. They beat me, they whip me, but it's ok.
Why is this not abuse, is there a way?

216. Put this in a bag,
and it becomes more lightweight.
But then the bag is no longer so great.

217. It is something the rich need,
but the poor already have.
If you eat it for a while,
your weight will drop by halve.

218. I tell you about your future.
The rich have me for sure.
I am a teller
and collected by a seller.

219. I have two arms and a neck but not a head.
I am obviously not a person,
what am I instead?

220. Eight of these protect the king.
Strong in the center and weak on the wing.

221. Hard to see, but I'm round in shape.
Past my horizon, there is no escape.
I bend the path of light with ease.
I always eat more without saying please.

222. I am a kind of tree, but I'm not alive.
From relationships, I do derive.

223. I wear many rings but not on a finger.
You have to look up to see where I linger.

224. I am always approaching but never arrive.
Always nearby, but I am not even alive.

225. Would you believe that water kills me,
but I am made of water, can you see?

226. A widget and a gadget together cost 1.10.
One buck more for the widget
than the gadget in money.
How much does a gadget cost?
The answer is funny.

227. If two people can paint
two walls in two hours,
how many walls can
four people paint in four hours?

228. I am an imperial monster with three feet.
     One foot on the left, one foot on the right,
     and one foot where they meet.

229. I cover your tooth.
     I cover your head.
     Rather than a hat,
     most want to wear this instead.

230. We work for the boss.
     I help you cast a spell.
     If you are old,
     I help you walk well.

231. I mark the field. I help you climb.
     I'm on a board. Solve this rhyme.

232. The walls of my room can be easily bent.
     Sleep overnight here, and you won't pay rent.

233. I am a king who measures things.
     If I hit your fingers, I am sure it stings.

234. You need me to drive around the city.
     I contain neither oil, gas, or electricity.

235. One for a saw, twice in a hammer,
     four for a wheelbarrow, and two on a ladder.

236. I can ruin a sword or puncture armor
     no matter how thick.
     However, I can't do much to a wooden stick.

237. As a baby, I fly. As a child, I lay flat.
After I die, I flow. Do you know?

238. A man who only breathes this in is soon dead,
but a plant can use it quite well instead.

239. You can not put me inside a pot,
but it keeps your food hot.

240. I never get older than a month old
but have been around a billion years.
When darkness lurks,
I ease your fears.

241. You call me an ear,
but I do not hear.

242. With me, most anything,
you can take a look inside.
Only by using lead,
from me, can you hide.

243. You can find us way up high.
First, we are wet, and then we are dry.
Our color can change, do you know why?

244. Once in June, twice for November,
three times in September.
How many in a calendar?

245. I am a game. I support a car.
Where your glasses rest, I am not far.

246. Scratch my head, and I will turn bright red.
     I go from cold to hot, then hot to dead.

247. A man jumps out of a plane
     without a parachute and survived.
     He landed without injury,
     when at the ground he arrived.
     How?

248. What does a vegetarian zombie like to eat?
     Here is a hint. It's not meat.

249. I flow forwards, but cannot be moved.
     My universal destiny remains unproved.

250. If you know what I am, then I am nothing.
     If you don't know me, then I am something.

251. I have a frame
     but hold no pictures nor any photos.
     I look near and far,
     but I am right beneath your nose.

252. Two halves joined together.
     When I'm upside down, I run much better.

253. I am exactly what I eat.
     This animal is really neat.

254. I can help you make food,
     but I don't taste good.
     My first half rhymes with my second half.
     My top half equals my bottom half.

255. With many uses for me, I am up to the task.
Once in place, I form a mask.
I hold on tightly from below.
Through my body, light can flow.

256. I do not belong in the following list:
cork, fork, pork, or stork.
Do you get the gist?

257. How is candy spelled with only two letters?
Yes, this puzzle has no errors.

258. I take a bow before I speak.
The sweeter my voice,
the greater of technique.

259. There was a plane crash
where every single person died,
but can you tell me who survived?

260. I can go from North to South,
but no words come out of my mouth.

261. Of them, it is shorter than the rest,
but signals that you think it's the best.

262. The first half is what you get when ice melts,
but I am food.
The second half is where you live,
and with pizza, I taste really good.

263. Red and black stones
   are used to play this game.
   Without these for facts,
   they are lies all the same.

264. I am certainly not alive,
   but if you use me, I will die.

265. We consist of visually striking sights
   and something that helps you see.
   I riddle you this,
   what can I be?

266. We play basketball well.
   We force a horse to go.
   I riddle you this, who am I?
   Do you know?

267. In this power outage during writing,
   you will certainly die.
   Now riddle me this,
   can you tell me why?

268. If you eat me, you will surely be eaten.
   Once we are together, there is no retreatin'.

269. When they are alive, we make our plans.
   When they are dead, we clap our hands.

270. I am made of wood,
   but you can't cut me with a saw.
   I know what you are thinking,
   but this riddle has no flaw.

271. You can buy me,
    but don't need me while you live.
    When you finally use me,
    you will have no review to give.

272. How do you subtract
    one from four to leave five?
    This mathematics is barely still alive.

273. Through this, you once did swallow,
    much later, I am just white and hollow.

274. I have a thousand legs,
    but on my own, I fall down.
    I am usually yellow or brown.

275. I bite down with two teeth,
    then I join whatever is beneath.

276. When I am quick, I am a threat.
    I surround the sea without a sweat.

277. They come from far away
    but are often not meant to stay.
    Most can't reach the earth
    for what they are worth.

278. Which plural English noun
    has three consecutive double letters?
    Here is a hint, they are service sellers.

279. I'm in the space outside,
     but to the eye, I hide.
     I speak your words.
     I am controlled by birds.

280. I really have only one eye.
     I see the future,
     so I know when I die.

281. I hold things inside,
     I and am one way you can lose your work.
     Often put in a bag by a shopping clerk.

282. I am a great coil.
     I move without oil.
     Steel or plastic,
     I am quite elastic.

283. In your drawer lie 11 socks,
     5 in green, 4 in blue, and 2 in red.
     If you want a matching pair out of 11,
     then what's the least that
     you should remove instead?

284. How many letters are there in
     an impossible riddle?
     It is the same as in
     the center and middle?

285. I am the part of a falcon that is not in the sky.
     I can swim in a lake, but easily remain dry.

286. I hold the world, so it does not fall.
     I contain many maps, but not them all.

287. This whistler indeed contains two T's.
At any given time, it makes any possible T.

288. Turn me around to get in or to get out.
I crack the code, what am I about?

289. When you need me, you throw me.
When you don't need me, you save me.

290. I fly without wings.
When I am done,
 you have had fun.

291. I am a square with stones for guts.
If you can't calculate, I will drive you nuts.

292. I am a type of tree,
as you will soon see.
I contain all five vowels that are possible,
but only seven letters, which are quite optimal.

293. There wouldn't be much privacy
in a room like this.
I contain the letter L three times in a row,
now can you guess?

294. You are given two fuses for dynamite
that last 10 minutes each,
stretched straight in the road.
How can you arrange the fuses and dynamite
so in 15 minutes it will explode?

295. A hole in my throat, a hole in my back.
I am known underwater to attack.

296. I can help you pay a bill.
My symmetry is greater even still.
A nine-letter word that does this math,
my top half matches my bottom half.

297. I am what you have when feeling good.
Invite me to this dance, you really should.

298. I go through your door
but hardly stay inside your house.
Once inside, I don't go out.
Lastly, I am smaller than a mouse.

299. My house is colored green,
but what's inside can't be seen.

300. Front to back and back to the right,
I am the same.
At this time, upside down or right side up
I still remain.

Answers

1. a comb
2. chewing gum
3. a sword
4. a Christmas tree
5. a pencil
6. wrong
7. darkness
8. a slide
9. a deck of cards
10. a needle
11. a coin
12. a parrot
13. a turkey
14. a table
15. the earth
16. a kangaroo

17	a sponge
18	a unicycle
19	a coat (as in a coat of paint)
20	a ring
21	ahead
22	an onion
23	a credit card
24	mistakenly
25	the letter c (sea)
26	a lighthouse
27	salt
28	weight
29	the stars
30	a tree
31	a book
32	pirates
33	a vacuum cleaner.

34 a glove

35 someone

36 a meatball

37 a pillow

38 legos

39 time

40 the truth

41 all 12 months have 28 days.

42 a keyboard

43 your shadow

44 a fence

45 a fan

46 a bottle

47 a newspaper

48 a storm

49 they weight the same

50 Tuesday, Thursday, today, tomorrow

51 a telescope

52 a noun

53 a treehouse

54 your name

55 baking soda

56 cookies

57 a season

58 a cloud

59 ropes

60 a fridge

61 the rain

62 the letter E

63 a beehive

64 WOW

65 suntan lotion

66 fire

67 a goldfish

68	a piano
69	a brush (tooth or hair)
70	a coffin
71	light
72	I live in the southern hemisphere
73	"seven" - s = even, and 7 - 1 = 6
74	a clock
75	small
76	a promise
77	the outdoors
78	a wheel
79	There is not dirt in empty space
80	water
81	a library
82	ton
83	a chainsaw
84	a snake

85	a blackboard
86	an address
87	and
88	DNA
89	a snail
90	electric trains don't make steam
91	a shamrock
92	the word wrong
93	a compass
94	horns
95	the letter "R"
96	breath
97	THEY SEE
98	a towel
99	wholesome
100	Carbon (diamonds are made of Carbon)
101	a dictionary

102 a toast

103 a baby shower

104 SILENT

105 a mountain

106 a six sided die

107 a deck of cards

108 an iceberg

109 a "palm" tree

110 a busboy

111 a crane

112 weight

113 on a clock

114 sevens

115 the letter E

116 a tree trunk

117 electricity

118 a shadow

119   a cold

120   he is still alive

121   a spine

122   the letter R

123   a pillow

124   an envelope

125   a stamp

126   a tree

127   a wristwatch

128   a painting

129   the letter W

130   a furnace

131   a vegetable

132   a dime and a nickel. A dime is not a nickel.

133   a pencil

134   the letter W

135   darkness

136   cymbals

137   the letter E

138   a mirror

139   the letter D

140   an egg

141   tree

142   BOOK (symmetrical about the middle of the word.)

143   a hamster on a wheel

144   a paper airplane

145   lightning

146   a headband

147   an umbrella

148   the letter T

149   He works at a barber shop.

150   a kiss (hershey's kiss)

151   an egg

152   a road

153   Donald is the son of his father.

154   Molly likes words with the same two letters next to each other, so she likes hammers.

155   a temper

156   a typewriter

157   the letter R

158   a parking garage

159   a base like in baseball

160   wax

161   a sand castle

162   a cell

163   a doorbell

164   the chair

165   a tongue

166   SOS

167   a scale

168   ink

169   a flag

170	your shadow
171	a bar of soap
172	5:15 = 17:15 in European time
173	a digital camera
174	history
175	zebra
176	a watermelon
177	a mummy
178	a rocket
179	a tree
180	a memory
181	ten -> net
182	a map
183	a doughnut
184	Acquire (A choir)
185	queue
186	You live on earth so the word is heart.

187 a secret

188 an address

189 whip

190 an echo

191 a mirror

192 a frisbee

193 a cell phone

194 an icicle

195 a veil

196   a laser

197 an egg

198 a cloud

199 insurance

200 chopsticks

201 the alphabet

202 silence

203 a t-shirt

204 organs

205 an ad-dress

206 your nose

207 a button

208 a duck

209 a plant

210 a peacock

211 there is an eclipse

212 BID. If you draw a horizontal line through the middle of the word it is the same on either side.

213 nose

214 light

215 preparing eggs

216 a hole

217 nothing

218 a fortune

219 a t-shirt

220 pawns in chess

221 a black hole

222 a family tree

223 Saturn

224 tomorrow

225 ice

226 The widget costs $1.05 and the gadget costs $0.05, 1.05 + 0.05 = 1.10

227 2x2x2 = 8 walls

228 a yardstick

229 a crown

230 a staff

231 chalk

232 a tent

233 a ruler

234 a driving license

235 Vowels "A" in a saw, "A" and "E" in a hammer, etc.

236 rust

237 snow

238 carbon dioxide

239 the lid

240 The moon (goes around the earth once a month).

241 an ear of corn

242 X-rays

243 leaves

244 one E in calendar. one E in June, etc.

245 a bridge

246 a match

247 The plane was on the ground and not flying

248 grains

249 time

250 a surprise party

251 reading glasses

252 an hourglass

253 an anteater

254   COOKBOOK. This word is symmetrical about a line drawn through its middle.

255   scotch tape

256   or

257   "C" and "Y"

258   a violin

259   couples and married people

260   a river

261   a thumb

262   mushrooms

263   checkers

264   a battery

265   spectacles

266   the spurs

267   skywriting

268   a fish hook

269   birthday candles

270   sawdust

271 a coffin

272 Roman numerals IV = 4, V=5.

273 a skull

274 a broom

275 a stapler

276 sand

277 asteroids

278 bookkeepers

279 the air

280 a cyclops

281 can (canned from your job)

282 slinky

283 four

284 "an impossible riddle" or "the center and middle" each have 18 letters.

285 a shadow

286 Atlas

287   a kettle

288   a key

289   an anchor

290   time flies when you are having fun

291   an abacus

292   SEQUOIA

293   wallless

294   Bend fuse 1 in half so the ends meet with the dynamite in the middle. Connect fuse 2 to the ends of fuse 1 and light the other end of fuse 2.

295   a killer whale

296   CHECKBOOK (a symmetrical word about its middle)

297   having a ball

298   a keyhole

299   a turtle

300   noon

One last thing. If you enjoyed this riddle book then please leave a review on Amazon. Authors like me rely on your support to sell books, and reviews definitely help. This link will take you there.

http://jmerrin.com/riddlesreview

If you find any errors or want to send me any feedback, you can reach me at

jackmerrin@gmail.com

You can check out some of my other best selling puzzle books.

1. Cryptograms: 200 LARGE PRINT Cryptogram Puzzles of Inspiration, Motivation, and Wisdom

2. Cryptograms #2: 250 Humorous LARGE PRINT Cryptoquote Puzzles

3. Cryptograms #3: 200 Philosophical LARGE PRINT Cryptoquote Puzzles

Thanks for you support, and I hope you enjoyed the book.

Made in the USA
Middletown, DE
16 November 2021